SEA MAMMALS

Written by *Anita Ganeri*
Illustrated by Denys Ovenden
and Malcolm McGregor

SIMON & SCHUSTER
YOUNG BOOKS

First published in 1993 by
Simon & Schuster Young Books
Simon & Schuster Limited
Campus 400
Maylands Avenue
Hemel Hempstead
Hertfordshire HP2 7EZ

Planned and produced by
Andromeda Oxford Limited
11-15 The Vineyard
Abingdon
Oxon OX14 3PX

ISBN 0-7500-1456-3
Printed in Singapore

Foreword

This book is about the different types of mammals that live most, or all, of their lives in or near the sea. Sea mammals include seals, sealions, whales and dolphins, polar bears and sea otters. Like other mammals, sea mammals are all warm-blooded animals that breathe air and feed their young on milk. However, their bodies have many special adaptations to help them survive in their watery, and sometimes very cold, homes.

Most sea mammals have a thick layer of fat, called blubber, under their skin. This helps to keep them warm and provides them with energy when food is scarce. Their bodies are also designed for swimming. Seals and whales, for example, have smooth, streamlined shapes for cutting through the water, and paddle-like flippers instead of legs. Sea otters and polar bears have webbed feet to help them swim.

Apart from polar bears and sea otters, there are three main groups of sea mammals. Whales, dolphins and porpoises are called cetaceans. Seals, sealions and walruses are called pinnipeds. Manatees and dugongs belong to the third and smallest group, the sirenians. These are also known as sea cows.

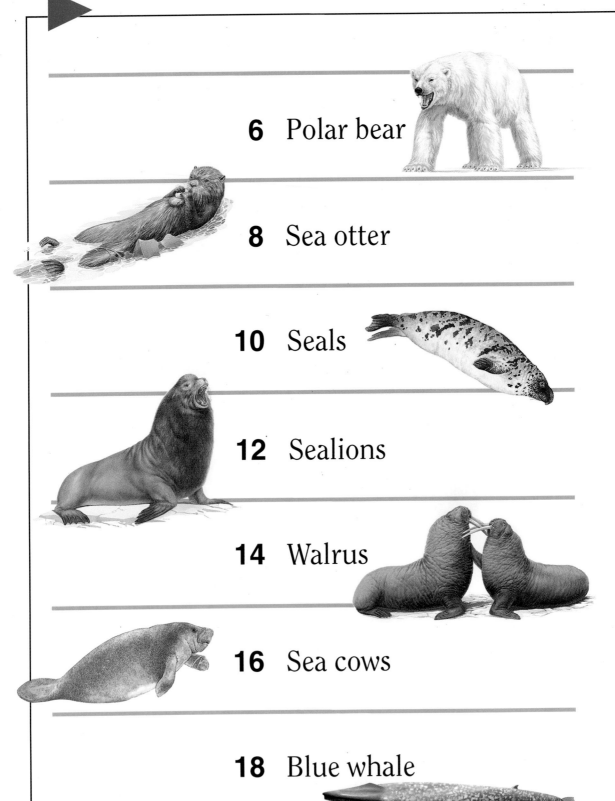

Contents

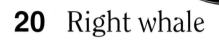

Polar bear

The polar bear is the biggest four-legged carnivore (meat-eater) in the world. It lives on the huge floating packs of ice which cover the Arctic Ocean. Sometimes the polar bear comes ashore, rummaging in town rubbish tips for food. But it prefers to float out to sea to hunt, using a large piece of ice as a raft.

The polar bear eats mainly seals, especially ringed seals. It catches them by waiting patiently by the seal's breathing hole in the ice. When the seal comes up for air, the bear pounces and kills the seal with a blow from its huge paws. The polar bear is also a superb swimmer. Its body is especially designed to help it survive both on the ice and in the water of its chilly home.

3 Animals can lose a lot of body heat through the skin on their ears (the temperature in the Arctic can fall as low as -50ºC). Polar bears have very small ears to stop too much precious heat being lost.

2 Polar bears have sharp, stabbing teeth for tearing and eating meat. As well as eating seals, they will also eat walruses and even small whales.

1 A polar bear has five long, sharp, curved claws on each foot. These help the bear to keep a firm grip on the slippery ice and to grab hold of prey.

4 Thick, white, waterproof fur keeps the polar bear warm and dry. It also makes the polar bear hard to spot among the ice and snow. This helps it to sneak up on prey without being seen.

Polar bear cubs are born in mid-winter in a snow den dug out by their mother. They stay in the den until spring, feeding on their mother's rich, fatty milk.

5 A polar bear's body is powerfully built. This helps make it a very strong swimmer and a ferocious hunter. Male bears are bigger than females. Adult male polar bears can weigh over half a tonne and stand 1.5m tall at the shoulders.

6 To help it swim, a polar bear has partly webbed feet. It uses its feet as paddles when swimming. It also has fur on the bottom of its feet to help it grip the ice.

►Sea otter

Sea otters spend most of their lives in the waters around the coast of California, USA. They even sleep at sea, wrapping strands of seaweed around their bodies to stop themselves drifting.

Sea otters are superb swimmers and divers. They catch clams, mussels, crabs, sea urchins and other seafood to eat. A sea otter has an ingenious way of opening up a clamshell to reach the meat inside. It lies on its back in the water, with a flat stone balanced on its chest. Then, holding the clam in its claws, it smashes the clam again and again against the stone until it cracks open. The otter eats the clam, then rolls over in the water to wash the bits of shell from its fur.

2 The sea otter's long, stiff whiskers help it to find food by sensing movements in the water. There are also sensitive whiskers on the sea otter's snout and elbows.

6 Sea otters have long, soft fur to keep them warm. About 100 years ago, they were almost hunted to extinction for their valuable fur.

1 The sea otter has webbed feet to help it swim. It can reach a top speed of about 9km/h in the water - almost twice as fast as your normal walking pace.

3 When the sea otter dives, it closes its nostrils and eyes to stop water entering. It usually dives for about a minute at a time.

4 Sea otters have strong teeth for crunching up their food. They eat a lot of food because they use up their energy very quickly.

5 The sea otter catches and opens it food with its front paws. Sometimes it must smash a clam against its stone 'table' 20 or more times to get the shell open.

Cape clawless otter

Oriental short-clawed otter

Like the sea otter, the oriental short-clawed otter and the Cape claw-less otter also grasp their prey in their front paws. Other kinds of otters catch their food in their mouths.

►Seals

Seals belong to the group of sea mammals called pinnipeds. The name means 'wing-footed' and describes the shape of the seals' flippers. Seals spend much of their lives in the water, chasing after fish to eat. They swim by using their webbed flippers to push themselves through the water. Seals are clumsy movers on land, but under water they are graceful swimmers. Seals can hold their breath for more than 30 minutes when they dive; they also close their nostrils to keep the water out.

Many seals live near the icy polar regions, so they need to keep warm. They all have oily, waterproof fur on their bodies. They also have a thick layer of fat, called blubber, under their skin which stops heat escaping from their bodies. Most seals have a layer of blubber up to 10cm thick.

pup

Harp seal
Northwest Atlantic

3 Hooded seals live in the Arctic and feed on squid and halibut. Although their teeth can grasp prey they cannot chew it, so the food is swallowed whole.

Hooded seal *Northern seas*

Crab-eater seal *Antarctic*

2 The leopard seal is a skilful hunter. It has sharp teeth, and eats penguins. It can swim very fast, and can also leap out of the water to land on the ice.

Leopard seal
Antarctic

1 Crab-eater seals have specially ridged teeth in their cheeks which they use for straining shrimp-like creatures, called krill, from the sea water.

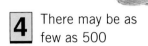

4 There may be as few as 500 Hawaiian monk seals left in the world, making it one of the rarest seals. The Caribbean monk seal may already be extinct.

5 Harp seal pups are born on the ice and have soft, white coats for warmth and camouflage. They moult (shed) their fur after about a month, and then grow a dark coat like the adults'.

Hawaiian monk seal
Northwest Hawaiian islands

6 The huge southern elephant seal is the biggest seal of all. The largest ever recorded was 6.5m long and weighed 4 tonnes.

To attract a mate, the male hooded seal inflates the lining of one nostril, making it look like a big, red balloon. This also warns rival males to keep away.

Southern elephant seal
Antarctic

Sealions

Sealions and fur seals are known as eared seals because they have tiny ear flaps. Their close relatives, the true seals (see pages 10 and 11) do not have ear flaps. Like true seals, however, sealions have sleek, streamlined bodies for moving easily through the water. They use their long front flippers like oars, and only use their back flippers for grooming their fur.

Californian sealions are very playful. They used to be kept in aquariums and circuses because they were so good at performing tricks. In the wild, they live on rocky islands off the coast of California, USA. Other sealions are found off the American and New Zealand coasts.

A sealion holds some air in its lungs as it dives. As it breathes out, it leaves a stream of bubbles behind.

2 A sealion has a coat of thick fur which is covered in oil to make it waterproof. Male Californian sealions have darker fur than females.

1 Sealions have a thick layer of blubber under their skin. This not only helps to keep them warm in the water but also makes their bodies more streamlined.

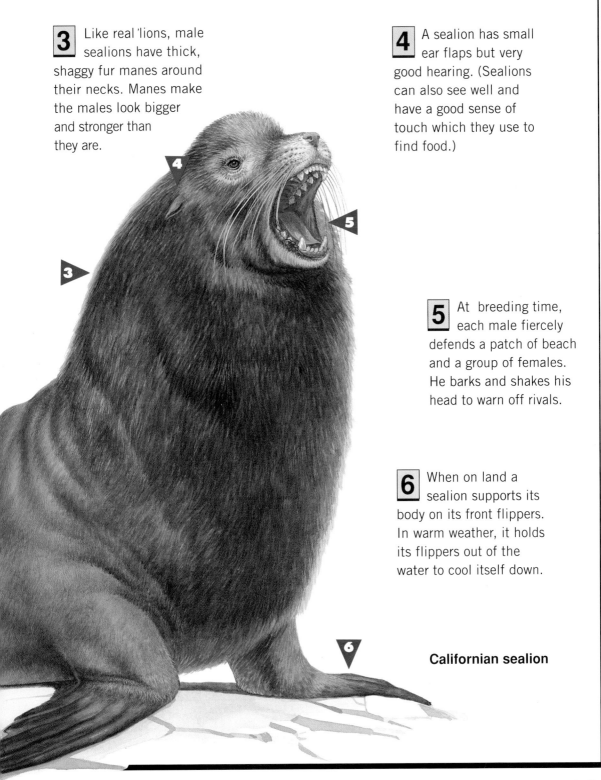

3 Like real lions, male sealions have thick, shaggy fur manes around their necks. Manes make the males look bigger and stronger than they are.

4 A sealion has small ear flaps but very good hearing. (Sealions can also see well and have a good sense of touch which they use to find food.)

5 At breeding time, each male fiercely defends a patch of beach and a group of females. He barks and shakes his head to warn off rivals.

6 When on land a sealion supports its body on its front flippers. In warm weather, it holds its flippers out of the water to cool itself down.

Californian sealion

►Walrus

Walruses live on the ice around the Arctic Ocean. They belong to the group of sea mammals known as pinnipeds, which includes seals, sealions and fur seals. Walruses live in large groups, or herds. In the breeding season, a herd may contain as many as a thousand walruses – bulls (males), cows (females) and calves (young). Newborn calves are about 1m long. An adult bull is four times this length.

Walruses are strong swimmers and hunt for their food on the seabed. They eat shellfish, sea urchins, crabs and fish. One walrus can eat as much as 45kg of food a day.

3 A walrus uses its snout like a spade for digging up food from the seabed. The walrus also squirts a jet of water from its mouth to blow away the sand and uncover shellfish.

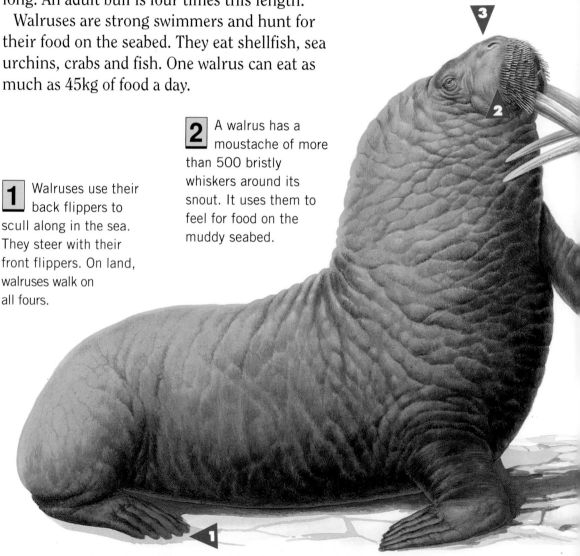

2 A walrus has a moustache of more than 500 bristly whiskers around its snout. It uses them to feel for food on the muddy seabed.

1 Walruses use their back flippers to scull along in the sea. They steer with their front flippers. On land, walruses walk on all fours.

4 Walrus tusks are actually very long canine teeth. A walrus uses its tusks to pull itself out of the sea, to break air holes in the ice and to defend itself. The walrus's scientific name - *Odobenus* - means 'tooth walker'.

A male walrus's tusks can grow up to 1m in length. Their size is an indication of a walrus's strength, age and importance in the herd. The male with the biggest tusks stands the best chance of attracting a female with which to mate.

5 A walrus's pink-brown skin is up to 4cm thick, and tough and leathery to give it protection. Walruses enjoy basking in the sun. Their skin turns pinker the longer they sunbathe, because their blood flows to the surface to absorb the warmth.

6 Male walruses have special air pouches in their throats. They inflate these to attract females and to help them float in the water.

Sea cows

'Sea cows' is the name given to the group of mammals which includes manatees and dugongs. They live in tropical rivers and in the warm shallow water along tropical coasts. These large, lumbering creatures graze on sea grasses and other water plants; in fact, they are the only sea mammals that feed almost entirely on plants.

Dugongs can grow to 4m in length and weigh almost a tonne. Manatees may weigh 1.5 tonnes. Both species can live for 50 years. Sadly, these gentle giants have been hunted almost to extinction for their skins and tasty meat. Their homes are also being destroyed by pollution. However, scientists have found that the animals are very useful because by feeding on water plants they clear the weeds which clog up some waterways. This may help to save them from being killed.

3 You can tell manatees and dugongs apart by their tails. A dugong's tail has pointed tips. A manatee's tail has rounded tips.

2 Manatees have very tiny ear holes but very good hearing. They use chirping and squeaking noises to talk to each other in the water.

1 A manatee has very long intestines for digesting the large amount of plants it eats daily – up to 1/4 tonne. Its intestines may be more than 45m long!

West African manatee
West African coasts

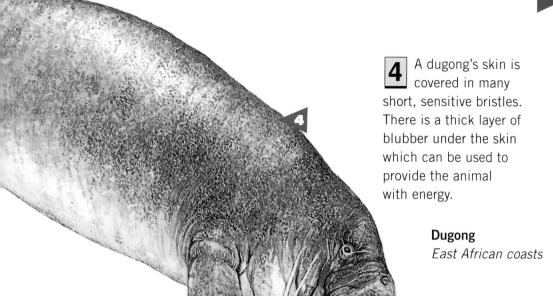

4 A dugong's skin is covered in many short, sensitive bristles. There is a thick layer of blubber under the skin which can be used to provide the animal with energy.

Dugong
East African coasts

5 The end of a dugong's snout is shaped rather like a horseshoe. It uses this part to forage for food on the seabed and pass it into its mouth.

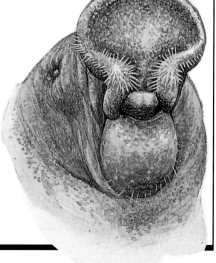

6 Manatees and dugongs do not have back flippers, only front flippers. They use their front flippers to dig out and carry food.

Manatees and dugongs have bristles on their lips which help them to feel their way in murky water. They have large, rubbery lips for pulling up grasses and water weeds.

Blue whale

3 Like all whales, the blue whale has to hold its breath when it dives. As it surfaces, it breathes the stale air out through the blowhole.

4 A blue whale's eyes are as big as footballs, although they seem small in relation to its gigantic body. Whales rely on sight and sound to find their prey.

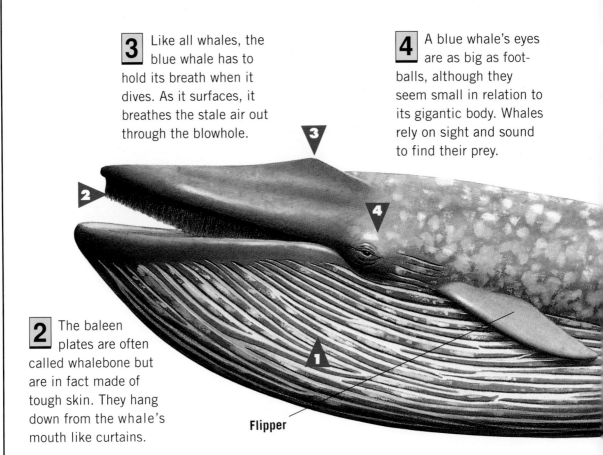

2 The baleen plates are often called whalebone but are in fact made of tough skin. They hang down from the whale's mouth like curtains.

Flipper

The blue whale is the biggest animal that has ever lived. Such a massive creature could not survive on land. Its legs would have to be so huge to support its body, that it would not be able to walk. In the sea, the water helps to support the body.

The blue whale roams the world's oceans, and eats tiny shrimps called krill. It can eat 4 tonnes of krill in one day. The blue whale does not have teeth. Instead it has plates, called baleen, hanging down from the roof of its mouth. The whale gulps in water containing krill and strains it out through the baleen. The krill are left behind and are then swallowed.

1 The blue whale has long grooves running down its throat. These allow it to open its mouth very wide when it is feeding. They also help it to move more freely through the water by reducing friction.

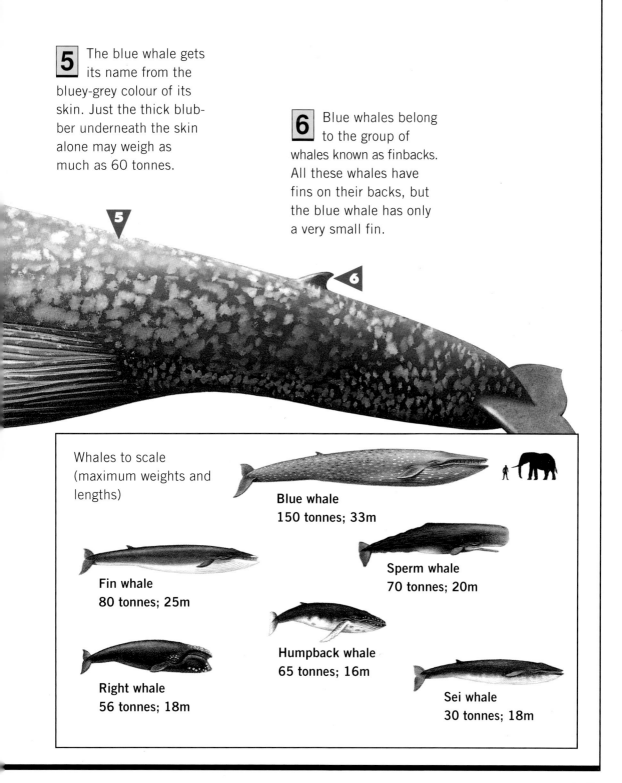

5 The blue whale gets its name from the bluey-grey colour of its skin. Just the thick blubber underneath the skin alone may weigh as much as 60 tonnes.

6 Blue whales belong to the group of whales known as finbacks. All these whales have fins on their backs, but the blue whale has only a very small fin.

Whales to scale (maximum weights and lengths)

Blue whale
150 tonnes; 33m

Fin whale
80 tonnes; 25m

Sperm whale
70 tonnes; 20m

Humpback whale
65 tonnes; 16m

Right whale
56 tonnes; 18m

Sei whale
30 tonnes; 18m

► Right whale ─────────

2 Right whales often slap their huge tails down on the water with a great crash. This behaviour is called 'lobtailing'.

1 The right whale's blubber was highly prized by hunters. They could get enough money from the blubber of one whale to pay for a whole whaling expedition.

There are three members of the right whale family – the right whale itself; the bowhead whale; and the pygmy right whale. The right whale may weigh 56 tonnes, while the pygmy right whale weighs just 3.5 tonnes. Like their close relatives the blue whales, right whales use their baleen to sieve tiny creatures from the sea water.

Right whales got their name because they were considered to be the right whales (that is, easy) for hunters to catch. They swam very slowly (about 5 km/h) and floated when they were killed. Like many other whales, they were killed for the oil obtained from their blubber and for their baleen. The oil was used in lamps, and the baleen was made into brush handles, combs and ladies' 'whalebone' corsets. So many right whales were hunted that they are now very rare.

Many whales can be identified by the size and shape of their 'spouts'. A spout is the air a whale breathes out.

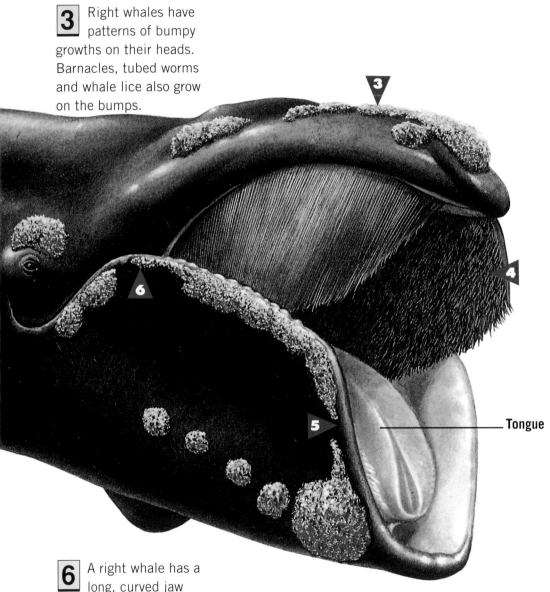

3 Right whales have patterns of bumpy growths on their heads. Barnacles, tubed worms and whale lice also grow on the bumps.

Tongue

6 A right whale has a long, curved jaw and a huge head, almost one third the length of its body. It sometimes lifts its head out of the water and bellows to tell other whales where it is.

5 Right whales swim near the surface with their mouths open. They skim their mouths over the water and strain out tiny animals to eat.

4 A right whale's baleen plates are about 2.5m long. It removes seaweed from the baleen with its tongue.

Sperm whale

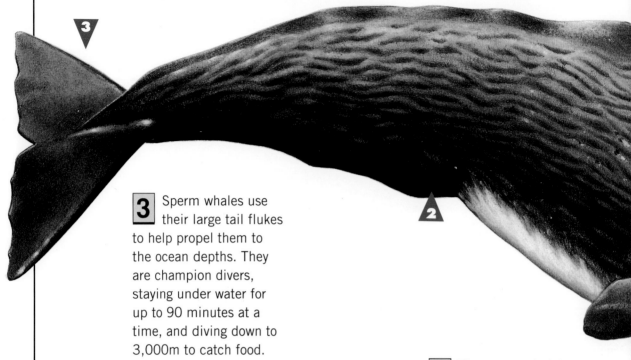

3 Sperm whales use their large tail flukes to help propel them to the ocean depths. They are champion divers, staying under water for up to 90 minutes at a time, and diving down to 3,000m to catch food.

2 The sperm whale's skin looks quite wrinkled and shrivelled. It is often marked, especially around the whale's head. These marks are made by squid suckers.

The sperm whale is the largest member of the group of whales known as toothed whales. Sperm whales are found in all seas, and hunt for their food in the inky blackness of the ocean depths. They probably rely on echolocation to help them find food. It is thought that they may also send out loud sounds to stun prey. Newborn sperm whales have no teeth, and some adults only have teeth in their bottom jaws. But this does not stop them eating large items of food, because it is usually swallowed whole.

Unlike most baleen whales, the male sperm whale (weighing up to 70 tonnes) is much bigger than the female (weighing up to 20 tonnes). Males migrate (travel) from the Equator to the Arctic and back each year. Females and young whales usually stay in the warmers seas.

1 The sperm whale feeds on deep-sea squid, like the one shown here. It also eats fish. A sperm whale may eat up to 1 tonne of squid a day.

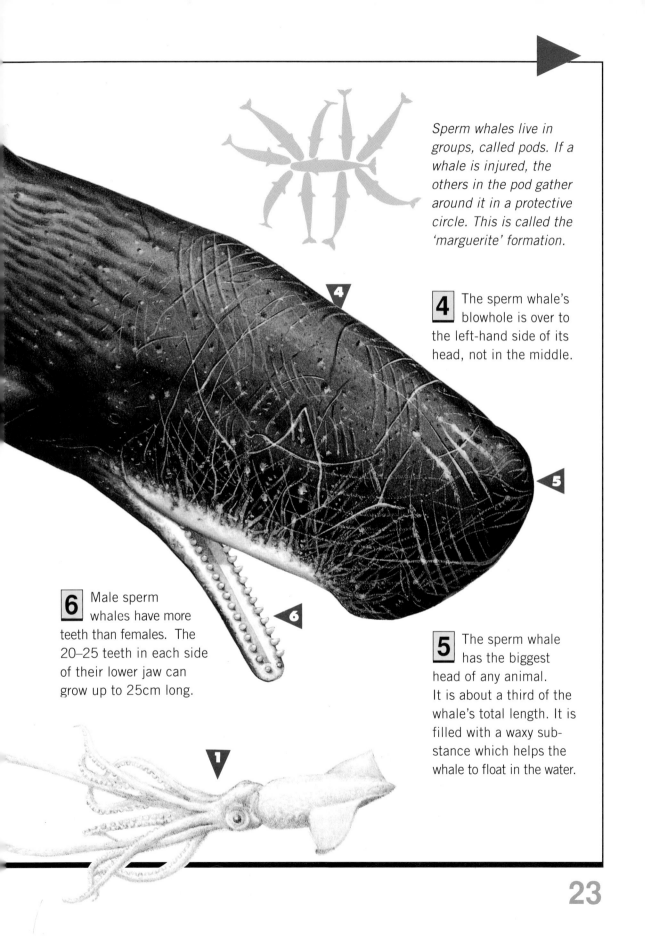

Sperm whales live in groups, called pods. If a whale is injured, the others in the pod gather around it in a protective circle. This is called the 'marguerite' formation.

4 The sperm whale's blowhole is over to the left-hand side of its head, not in the middle.

6 Male sperm whales have more teeth than females. The 20–25 teeth in each side of their lower jaw can grow up to 25cm long.

5 The sperm whale has the biggest head of any animal. It is about a third of the whale's total length. It is filled with a waxy substance which helps the whale to float in the water.

White whales

The white whale family has just two members – the narwhal and the beluga. Both live in the Arctic Ocean, and both have striking appearances. Adult belugas are pure white in colour. They swim in small groups, often working together to herd fish into the shallow water where they are easier to catch.

Narwhals swim in herds too. Each male has an extraordinary spiralling tusk. This develops from one of the narwhal's teeth. No one is quite sure what narwhals use their tusks for. Rival males may use them as jousting weapons when they compete for females, or they may just be for ornament. In the past, people killed narwhals to sell their tusks, pretending that they were the horns of a mythical animal called a unicorn.

2 Newborn belugas are brownish-red in colour. After a year, they turn grey. By the time they are five years old, they are pure white.

1 The male narwhal's tusk can grow to 2.5m long. It grows through the narwhal's lip from the left of its top jaw, in an anti-clockwise spiral.

Narwhal *male*
Arctic

Beluga
1 year old

3 Unlike most whales, a beluga has a very flexible neck. It can turn it almost at a right angle in order to look sideways.

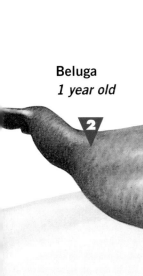

4 Belugas are nick-named 'sea canaries' because they make so many different noises. They chirp, whistle and click, and clap their jaws together.

Beluga *adult*
Arctic

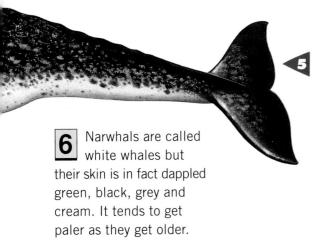

5 As a male narwhal gets older, its tail changes shape. The tips grow forwards so that the tail looks as if it is back to front.

6 Narwhals are called white whales but their skin is in fact dappled green, black, grey and cream. It tends to get paler as they get older.

Dolphins

There are 32 species of dolphin, living in seas all over the world. The killer whale is the biggest dolphin. The bottle-nosed dolphin is famous for its intelligence and playfulness.

Dolphins are small, toothed whales (see pages 22–23). Most have 100 to 200 sharp, pointed teeth which are used for catching slippery fish. Most dolphins also have a beak-like nose, a fin on their back and a round bump on their forehead. They use echolocation to find food and navigate under water. They make lots of clicking sounds, but they are too high-pitched for humans to be able to hear. If the sounds hit something, they send back an echo. From this, the dolphins can tell what lies ahead.

3 The killer whale has a huge, triangular fin on its back. This can stand 2m high - as big as a tall person. No other species of whale has a bigger fin.

2 Killer whales hunt and eat fish, sharks, squid and even seals, porpoises and walruses. But they do not eat people, despite their name!

1 Dolphins have streamlined bodies for fast swimming. The killer whale is the fastest of all sea mammals. It can reach a top speed of about 65km/h.

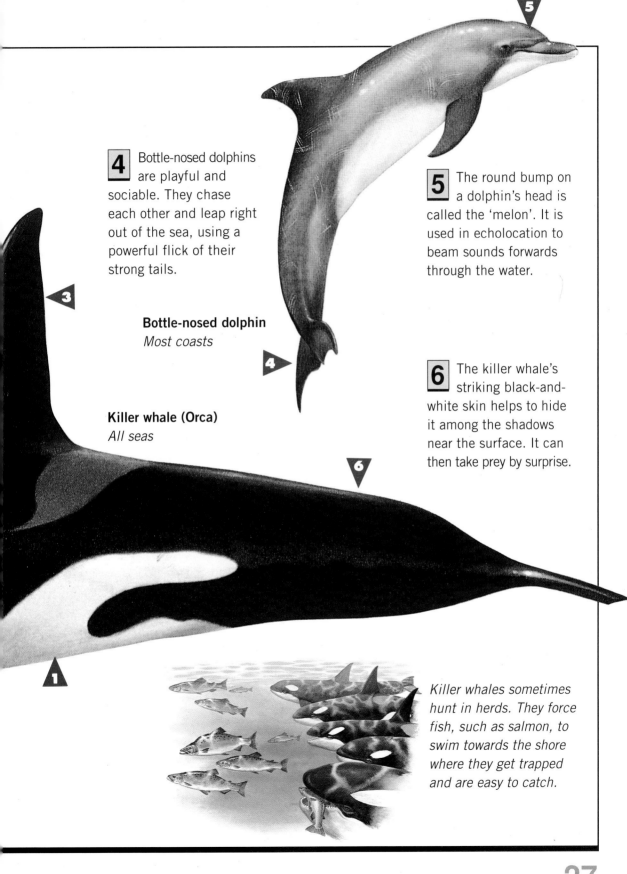

4 Bottle-nosed dolphins are playful and sociable. They chase each other and leap right out of the sea, using a powerful flick of their strong tails.

Bottle-nosed dolphin
Most coasts

Killer whale (Orca)
All seas

5 The round bump on a dolphin's head is called the 'melon'. It is used in echolocation to beam sounds forwards through the water.

6 The killer whale's striking black-and-white skin helps to hide it among the shadows near the surface. It can then take prey by surprise.

Killer whales sometimes hunt in herds. They force fish, such as salmon, to swim towards the shore where they get trapped and are easy to catch.

27

Porpoises

Porpoises look quite similar to dolphins. Like dolphins, they are a type of very small whale. But they are usually even smaller than dolphins, rarely growing more than 2m in length, and they do not have 'beaks' on their heads. They do use echolocation, however, to find their food of fish, shellfish and squid. They also use a selection of sounds, such as grunts, clicks and squeaks to communicate with each other.

Porpoises live along the coast and in river estuaries. They are fast, strong swimmers, using their tails to propel themselves along.

3 Burmeister's porpoise has a blackish grey back and sides, with a paler underside.

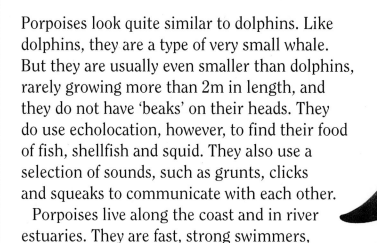

2 Dall's porpoise often has tiny plants growing on the back of the fin and flippers. This sometimes makes them look slightly yellow in colour.

Dall's porpoise
Pacific coasts of North America and northern Europe

1 As its name suggests, the finless porpoise has no fin on its back. Young finless porpoises sometimes ride piggy-back on their mothers.

Finless porpoise
Indo-Pacific coasts

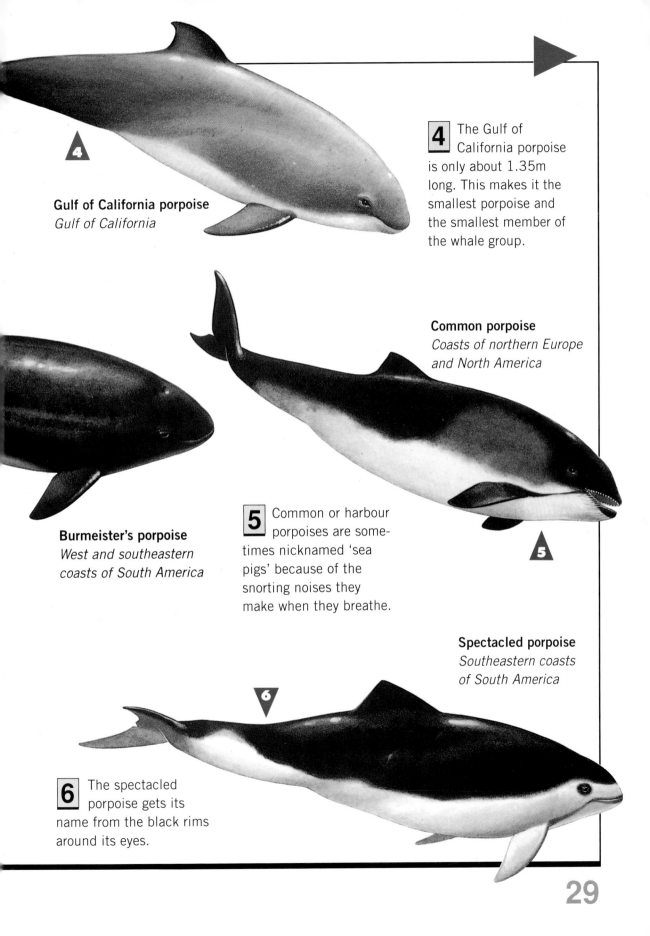

Gulf of California porpoise
Gulf of California

4 The Gulf of California porpoise is only about 1.35m long. This makes it the smallest porpoise and the smallest member of the whale group.

Common porpoise
Coasts of northern Europe and North America

Burmeister's porpoise
West and southeastern coasts of South America

5 Common or harbour porpoises are sometimes nicknamed 'sea pigs' because of the snorting noises they make when they breathe.

Spectacled porpoise
Southeastern coasts of South America

6 The spectacled porpoise gets its name from the black rims around its eyes.

►Glossary

Adaptations
Special features which help an animal to survive in its particular home. These may include thick fur to keep animals warm in cold places.

Baleen
Horny plates which hang down from the roof of some whales' mouths. The edges of the plates are fringed. They act like giant sieves to filter food out of sea water. Baleen is actually tough skin, not bone.

Barnacle
A kind of crustacean that lives attached to rocks, ships and the skin of whales.

Beak
A dolphin's long, slender beak-like snout.

Blowhole
The single or double hole on top of a whale's or dolphin's head. It is actually the animal's nostrils. The shape of the spray of exhaled (breathed out) air is different in each type of whale or dolphin.

Blubber
A thick layer of fat under an animal's skin. It helps to keep it warm and can be used as a source of food.

Bonnet
The bumpy growths found on top of a right whale's head. Like our fingerprints, the pattern of the bonnet is unique to each whale.

Camouflage
Special markings or colouring which help to hide an animal.

Carnivore
An animal that mainly, or only, eats meat.

Cetacean
A member of the group of sea mammals which includes whales and dolphins. Cetaceans have streamlined bodies, flippers instead of front limbs and a tail with large flukes to drive them through the water.

Dolphin
A small member of the cetacean group. It usually has a beak-like snout.

Echolocation
A method of finding food and navigating by using sound. It is used by dolphins, porpoises and some whales.

Extinct
The word used to describe an animal or plant that has died out and no longer exists.

Flexible
Something that is easy to bend.

Flipper
The limb of a seal, whale or dolphin that is shaped like a paddle for swimming.

Fur seal
A close relative of the sealions. Like sealions, fur seals have ear flaps and walk on all fours when on land. They have thicker fur coats than sealions.

Inflate
To blow up like a balloon.

Krill
Small sea animals that are related to shrimps. They live in vast swarms and are the staple diet of blue whales.

Lobtailing
A type of behaviour found in right whales in which they bring their tails crashing down on the water.

Mammal
A warm-blooded animal that breathes air and feeds its babies on milk. Most mammals give birth to live young.

Marguerite formation
The pattern made by a group of sperm whales when they gather around an injured member of their pod. They form a circle, heads pointing inwards and tails outwards. They look rather like the petals on a marguerite flower.

Melon
The rounded bump on a dolphin's forehead. It helps to beam sounds forward during echolocation.

Migrate
To make long, regular journeys between breeding and feeding places at particular times of the year.

Navigate
To find the way, especially in the water.

Pinniped
A member of the group of sea mammals which includes seals, sealions and walruses.

Pod
Name given to a group of dolphins or whales.

Porpoise
The smallest member of the cetacean group. Porpoises have shorter, rounder snouts than dolphins.

Prey
Animals that are hunted by others for food.

Seal
A member of the pinnipeds closely related to the sealions and fur seals. Seals do not have ear flaps.

Sealion
A close relative of the fur seals. Like fur seals, sealions have ear flaps and walk on all fours when on land.

Sirenian
A member of the group of sea mammals which includes the manatees and the dugongs.

Species
A group of animals that are of the same kind. They look alike and behave in similar ways. They are able to breed with each other but not with other species.

Streamlined
Describes a shape which is smooth, sleek and torpedo-shaped for easy movement through water or the air.

Tail flukes
The two flattened tips of the tail of a whale or dolphin. They provide the power needed for swimming.

Whale
Any of the members of the cetacean group of sea mammals.

Whalebone
Another name for the baleen of whales.

Whale lice
Small crustaceans that infest whales.

► Index